# *Nita Mehta's*
# Chinese
## Cooking

## *Nita Mehta's*

B.Sc. (Home Science), M.Sc. (Food and Nutrition), Gold Medalist

*Nita Mehta's*

# Chinese
## Cooking

ISBN 81-7869-158-2

*Exclusive Distributor:*

**AMPRODUCTIONS**
DIVISION OF: INFORMATION SCIENCE INDUSTRIES (CANADA) LIMITED

1169 Parisien St., Ottawa, Ont., K1B 4W4,
Tel: 613.745.3098 Fax: 613.745.7533
e-mail: amproductions@rogers.com
web: www.amproductions.ca

*Published by:*

**SNAB**

**Publishers Pvt. Ltd.**
**3A/3 Asaf Ali Road,**
**New Delhi - 110002**
Tel: 23252948, 23250091
Telefax:91-11-23250091
**INDIA**

*Editorial and Marketing office:*
E-159, Greater Kailash-II, N.Delhi-48
*Fax:*91-11-29225218, 29229558
*Tel:*91-11-29214011, 29218727, 29218574
*E-Mail:* nitamehta@email.com, nitamehta@nitamehta.com
*Website:*http://www.nitamehta.com
*Website:* http://www.snabindia.com

*Printed at:*
PRESSTECH LITHO PVT LTD, NEW DELHI

**Price: $ 5.95**

# Contents

## appetizers    12

## dry & stir fried    34

## saucy dishes    22

## dessert    46

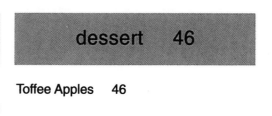

# Introduction

Chinese food offers you complex and lively flavours: sweet, sour, hot, tangy, piquant and salty. There is a texture contrast between crisp and smooth. The vegetables are always brightly coloured.

Keeping these requirements in mind the recipes have been arranged in an orderly manner to achieve the desired results. In order to retain the colour and crunch of vegetables they have to be cut correctly, exposing the maximum surface to help them to cook faster, which keeps them crunchy.

I have given a special section on techniques for cutting vegetables and information on special equipment, ingredients and sauces used in Chinese cooking. Enjoy the taste of China, all cooked in a simple manner in your own kitchen!

Nita Mehta

# INTERNATIONAL CONVERSION GUIDE

*These are not exact equivalents; they've been rounded-off to make measuring easier.*

## WEIGHTS & MEASURES

| METRIC | IMPERIAL |
|--------|----------|
| 15 g | ½ oz |
| 30 g | 1 oz |
| 60 g | 2 oz |
| 90 g | 3 oz |
| 125 g | 4 oz (¼ lb) |
| 155 g | 5 oz |
| 185 g | 6 oz |
| 220 g | 7 oz |
| 250 g | 8 oz (½ lb) |
| 280 g | 9 oz |
| 315 g | 10 oz |
| 345 g | 11 oz |
| 375 g | 12 oz (¾ lb) |
| 410 g | 13 oz |
| 440 g | 14 oz |
| 470 g | 15 oz |
| 500 g | 16 oz (1 lb) |
| 750 g | 24 oz (1½ lb) |
| 1 kg | 30 oz (2 lb) |

## LIQUID MEASURES

| METRIC | IMPERIAL |
|--------|----------|
| 30 ml | 1 fluid oz |
| 60 ml | 2 fluid oz |
| 100 ml | 3 fluid oz |
| 125 ml | 4 fluid oz |
| 150 ml | 5 fluid oz (¼ pint/1 gill) |
| 190 ml | 6 fluid oz |
| 250 ml | 8 fluid oz |
| 300 ml | 10 fluid oz (½ pint) |
| 500 ml | 16 fluid oz |
| 600 ml | 20 fluid oz (1 pint) |
| 1000 ml | 1¾ pints |

## CUPS & SPOON MEASURES

| METRIC | IMPERIAL |
|--------|----------|
| 1 ml | ¼ tsp |
| 2 ml | ½ tsp |
| 5 ml | 1 tsp |
| 15 ml | 1 tbsp |
| 60 ml | ¼ cup |
| 125 ml | ½ cup |
| 250 ml | 1 cup |

## HELPFUL MEASURES

| METRIC | IMPERIAL |
|--------|----------|
| 3 mm | 1/8 in |
| 6 mm | ¼ in |
| 1 cm | ½ in |
| 2 cm | ¾ in |
| 2.5 cm | 1 in |
| 5 cm | 2 in |
| 6 cm | 2½ in |
| 8 cm | 3 in |
| 10 cm | 4 in |
| 13 cm | 5 in |
| 15 cm | 6 in |
| 18 cm | 7 in |
| 20 cm | 8 in |
| 23 cm | 9 in |
| 25 cm | 10 in |
| 28 cm | 11 in |
| 30 cm | 12 in (1ft) |

## HOW TO MEASURE

When using the graduated metric measuring cups, it is important to shake the dry ingredients loosely into the required cup. Do not tap the cup on the table, or pack the ingredients into the cup unless otherwise directed. Level top of cup with a knife. When using graduated metric measuring spoons, level top of spoon with a knife. When measuring liquids in the jug, place jug on a flat surface, check for accuracy at eye level.

## OVEN TEMPERATURE

These oven temperatures are only a guide. Always check the manufacturer's manual.

| | °C (Celsius) | °F (Fahrenheit) | Gas Mark |
|--|-----------|--------------|----------|
| Very low | 120 | 250 | 1 |
| Low | 150 | 300 | 2 |
| Moderately low | 160 | 325 | 3 |
| Moderate | 180 | 350 | 4 |
| Moderately high | 190 | 375 | 5 |
| High | 200 | 400 | 6 |
| Very high | 230 | 450 | 7 |

# Chinese Ingredients and Sauces

*Before actual cooking, check if you have all the necessary sauces and seasonings. There are several items that are important in Chinese cooking, e.g. soya sauce, vinegar, cornstarch etc. These essentials will help you create authentic flavours. Start with a few basic items.*

### SOYA SAUCE:

There are 2 kinds. One is dark and the other is light. Both are used for seasoning foods. It cannot be made at home. It is easily available in bottles in grocery shops.

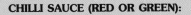

### VINEGAR:

It may be synthetic (acetic acid) or prepared from natural ingredients like rice, wine, sugar, fruits etc. The natural ones are better as the synthetically prepared chemical ones are too tart.

### CHILLI SAUCE (RED OR GREEN):

This is a hot, spicy and tangy sauce made from red or green chillies, vinegar and seasonings. It is available ready made.

### BLACK BEAN SAUCE:

This sauce is made from fermented black beans. It has a pungent and salty flavour. It cannot be made at home. It is available ready made in bottles at shops.

### HOISIN SAUCE:

Also called peking or barbecue sauce. This thick brownish-red sauce is made form soya beans, spices, garlic and chilli peppers. It is used both in cooking and as a condiment. It is available ready made in bottles.

### WORCESTERSHIRE SAUCE:

It is a thin dark, piquant sauce used to season dishes. It is made from tamarind, dry fruits, garlic, ginger and spices.

### OYSTER SAUCE:

Made from fresh oysters. Its special aroma and subtle sweetness enhance the flavours of most dishes. It is used not only in cooking but also as a condiment. Sprinkle a few drops over stir-fried iceberg lettuce & you will love it. Available in bottles & cans, it is best to refrigerate after opening.

### SESAME OIL:

It is used as a flavouring, but not usually for cooking. It has a strong distinctive nutty taste & fragrant aroma. Only a small quantity is required. In cooked dishes a few drops of oil are usually added just prior to serving. It adds flavour to dips, salads and stir fry dishes.

## STAR ANISE *(Chakri Phool)*:

The dried, hard, brown, star shaped fruit has a fennel flavour. It is an important ingredient used in five spice powder. It can be substituted with fennel seeds.

## FIVE SPICE POWDER:

An aromatic blend of 5 Oriental spices: 2 tsp peppercorns (*saboot kali mirch*), 3 star anise (*phool chakri*), 6 cloves (*laung*), 4" stick cinnamon (*dalchini*) and 3 tsp fennel (*saunf*). It is slightly sweet and pungent. Grind together to a powder, sieve & use.

## CORNSTARCH:

It is a white powder, which is used to thicken sauces. Dissolve some cornstarch in little tap water to make a paste and add it to boiling liquid. Remember to stir the sauce continuously, when the paste is being added.

## BEAN CURD/TOFU:

It is prepared from soya bean milk. There is firm tofu which is good for stir frying, where as the soft silken tofu is added as it is to dishes. Tofu resembles Indian Paneer in taste & looks.

## SNOW PEAS/MANGETOUT:

They belong to the pea family and are used in cooking just like we use green beans. Whole pod is edible. Snap off the stem end of pea pod and pull the thread.

## DRY RED CHILLI:

Dry red chillies are easily available in markets. They are really hot. You can deseed them to decrease their heat.

## CHINESE WINE:

There are many kinds of wine made from rice. Chinese wine can be substituted by ordinary dry sherry. Small amount of this wine adds a mild flavor.

## SESAME SEEDS (TIL):

These tiny, teardrop-shaped, flat seeds are quite tasteless in their raw state but impart a wonderful nutty flavour after roasting. These are cream and black in colour. The taste and visual appeal of food is enhanced, when coated with these seeds.

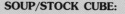

## SOUP/STOCK CUBE:

Stock is an important agent for most soups and sauces. However, if you do not have stock ready or feel lazy to make a stock, you can use stock cubes mixed in water instead. Stock cubes are available as small packets. These are very salty, so taste the dish after adding the cube before you put more salt. Always crush the cube to a powder before using it.

## GREEN ONIONS (*HARA PYAZ*):

These are also called scallions or spring onions. In the absence of these, you can substitute them with regular onions. The green and white part, both are used. Add green part just at the end of cooking.

## BAMBOO SHOOTS:

Fresh tender shoots of Bamboo plant are available rarely, but tinned bamboo shoots are easily available.

## AGAR-AGAR:

This is a dried seaweed. The white fibrous strands can be crushed to a powder in a small grinder. It requires soaking and is used like gelatine. It is used for puddings and as a setting agent.

## BEAN SPROUTS:

These are shoots of moong beans or soya beans. The texture is crisp.

To make bean sprouts at home, soak ½ cup of green beans (*saboot moong dal*) for about 8 hours. Discard water and tie in a muslin cloth. Keep them tied for 2-3 days, remembering to wet the cloth each day. When the shoots are long enough, wash carefully in water. Fresh bean sprouts will keep for 3-4 days if refrigerated in a plastic bag.

## CHINESE CABBAGE  (wongnga bak/napa cabbage):

It looks like a tightly packed cos lettuce. It has firm, pale green, crinkled leaves. If unavailable, ordinary cabbage can be used.

## BOK CHOY (CHINESE CHARD):

A variety of Chinese cabbage. Also called spoon cabbage. It has dark green leaves with a white stalk and is used for stir frying. Both stalk and the leaves can be used. It is cooked only for a minute, so that it retains its colour and texture.

## OYSTER MUSHROOMS:

These soft mushrooms are shaped like a fan. Delicious in flavour. Use them as soon as possible. Store in fridge. Available in dried form also.

## DRIED MUSHROOMS:

May be white or black. To prepare dried mushrooms for cooking, soak them in hot water for at least ½ hour to soften. They swell in size after soaking. Discard any hard stems. Cut into required size and use. They harbour a lot of dust and grit, so it is necessary to wash them well after soaking. They are  added to dishes only for the last few minutes of cooking, to retain the crunchy texture. Used in soups and stir-fries.

# Chinese Cooking Utensils

Before actual cooking, check if you have all the necessary utensils. There are several items that are indispensable in Chinese cooking, e.g. wok and wok strainer etc. These essentials will help you create authentic flavours. Start with a few basic items.

## WOK:

It is a deep pan, round bottomed with a single or double handle on the sides. A wok is ideal not only for stir-frying but deep-frying and simmering also. Chinese cook everything in a wok - from soups to rice to main course dishes. Choose a heavy bottomed one. Non stick woks are also available.

The wok comes in various sizes, the bigger the better.  The most functional size is the 11-12 inch (28- 30 cm) round wok. Sometimes it's fitted with a lid and an inner rack so you can steam vegetables and fish in it. The wok is deep, so you can boil rice and make soup in it. Its rounded sides provide enough red-hot surface for stir-frying foods quickly, usually in 3 to 5 minutes. The Indian *kadhai* is similar to a wok. You can use it in the absence of a wok. But , buying a Chinese wok is much worth the investment!

## WOK STRAINER:

A special strainer used to remove deep-fried pieces of food all together from oil at one time. Also useful for blanching food in hot water. Choose one which is slightly smaller than the wok. If not available, substitute with a single handle metal strainer.

## STEAMING RACK (BAMBOO BASKETS):

An essential tool for steaming food, made of bamboo which allows steam  to rise efficiently. Place the steamer basket on a wok with ½" of boiling water as a single steamer or stack in several tiers so various dishes can be steamed at a time.

## LADLE:

Perfect for stir-frying and braising any food in a wok. The preferred ladle has a sturdy joint and an easy-to-hold handle.

## CHOPPING BOARD:

The Chinese use a big heavy chopping board on which they chop almost everything with a broad flat knife. An ordinary board of a moderate size can be used.

## CHOPSTICKS:

These are thin long sticks, generally made of wood, and are used by the Chinese to eat with as well as to stir food while cooking.

# Vegetable Cutting Methods

**CHOPPING: TO CUT INTO SMALL PIECES**

The vegetable is cut into small pieces. Holding on to the vegetable firmly, cut the vegetable lengthwise into slices and then holding on firmly, give  the sliced vegetable a quick turn at a right angle. Now cut the sliced vegetable again into slices which will result in finely chopped pieces. Onions and tomatoes are usually chopped in the recipes.

**DIAGONAL SLICES: TO CUT VEGETABLE SLICES IN A SLANTING MANNER**

The vegetables are cut into thin slices in a slanting manner in such a way that there are more exposed surfaces. Vegetables such as asparagus, carrots, celery or green beans are usually diagonally sliced.

**SLICING: TO CUT COMPLETELY THROUGH THE VEGETABLE TO GET SLICES**

The vegetables are cut into thin slices. The thickness depends on what is specified in each individual recipe. Tomatoes, carrots,  mushrooms, onions etc. are sliced in quite a few recipes.

**SHREDDING: TO CUT INTO THIN, LONG PIECES**

The vegetables are cut into thin strips or shreds. Spinach, lettuce, cabbage are all shredded. Carrot can  be grated on the big holes of a grater to get shredded carrot.

 **DICING: TO CUT INTO VERY SMALL SQUARES**

The vegetables are cut into dice or small cubes. The vegetables are first cut lengthwise into ¼ or ½ inch thick strips/fingers and several such strips/fingers are kept together and further cut into ¼ inch pieces.

**JULLIENE: TO CUT INTO THIN MATCH STICK LIKE PIECES**

The vegetables are cut into thin slices lengthwise. The slices are stacked together and cut lengthwise to get thin match sticks. Carrots and cucumber juliennes look good.

**RINGS AND HALF RINGS: TO CUT THE VEGETABLES WIDTHWISE INTO ROUNDS**

Vegetables like onions or bell peppers are cut widthwise to get rounds. The onion slices are then separated to give full rings.  For half rings, cut the vegetables first into half and then cut widthwise to get half rings. When opened the half rings look like thin strips of onion and can be used as shredded onion also.

## CARROT OR RADISH FLOWERS:

These flowers are usually seen in Chinese dishes. If the dish requires  round slices of carrots, cut the carrot into round flowers instead. It enhances the look of stir fried dishes.

For carrot flowers, peel a thick, big carrot. Cut into two pieces to get 2 shorter lengths. Firmly holding the carrot upright, with a small sharp knife, make 1/8 inch broad and deep lengthwise cuts along the length of the carrot. Tilt the knife slightly to take out the thin long piece from the cut to get a groove. Make 2-3 more grooves leaving equal space between them. Carefully, cut the carrot into round slices.

## CARROT LEAVES:

### CUT A CARROT INTO VERY SLANTING SLICES.

Cut a big carrot into very thin and very slanting slices. Make "V" notches on the side to get leaves.

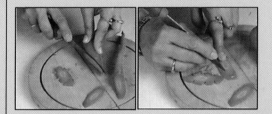

**TRIANGULAR PIECES:** cut a bell pepper into 4 pieces lengthwise. Cut each piece at an angle, to get a small triangle of about 1". Cut the left over strip into half, giving a slant cut in the opposite direction at the centre to get 2 more triangles. Similarly you could get triangular pieces of tomatoes also. Coloured bell peppers really look good when cut into this shape.

# Appetizers

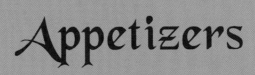

# Sweet Corn Vegetable Soup

*The best known and best loved Chinese soup of all time! No need to go to a restaurant when you get the craving for your favourite soup!*

*Serves 4*

## INGREDIENTS

1 cup cream style sweet corn, canned
4 cups stock/broth/water
1 tbsp oil
¼ cup finely chopped carrot
¼ cup finely chopped cabbage
2-3 green beans - very finely chopped
½ tsp green chilli sauce
½ tsp red chill sauce
1 tbsp vinegar, ¼ tsp pepper
1 tsp level salt, or to taste
½ tsp sugar, or to taste
1 tsp light soya sauce
5 tbsp cornstarch dissolved in ¾ cup water

## METHOD

1 Mix cream style corn with 4½ cups water in a deep pan. Bring to a boil. Boil for 5 minutes.

2 Add chilli sauces and vinegar. Simmer for 1-2 minutes.

3 Meanwhile heat 1 tbsp oil in a nonstick pan, add the vegetables. Saute for 1 minute. Add the sauteed vegetables to the simmering soup. Simmer for 1 minute.

4 Add salt, sugar and pepper to the soup.

5 Add cornstarch paste and cook for 2-3 minutes till the soup thickens. Add just a little soya sauce, taking care not to discolour the soup. Serve hot.

### TiP

**Sweet Corn Soup with Fresh Corn**

*For fresh corns, grate 5 large corns and pressure cook grated corn with 9 cups water and 1½ tbsp sugar to give 2 whistles. Keep on low heat for 6-7 minutes. Remove from heat and let it cool down. Proceed from step 2.*

# Hot & Sour Soup

*You can get addicted to the heady excitement of this soup! To make a non-vegetarian version boil 200 g chicken with the bones, in 6 cups of water till chicken is tender, about 7-8 minutes. Use the chicken liquid instead of the water in the recipe. Debone boiled chicken and shred into small pieces and add along with the vegetables. You may omit the mushrooms.*

*Serves 4-5*

## METHOD

1. If dried mushrooms are available, soak them in water for ½ hour to soften. Wash thoroughly to clean the dirt in them. Cut away any hard portion and then cut into smaller pieces.

2. Heat 2 tbsp oil. Add chilli paste and garlic. Give it a quick stir.

3. Add beans and mushrooms. Stir fry for 1-2 minutes on high heat. Add cabbage and carrots. Stir for a few seconds.

4. Add 5 cups water and the soup/stock cubes. Add sugar, salt, pepper, soya sauce, vinegar and ketchup. Boil for 2 minutes.

5. Add cornstarch paste, stirring continuously. Cook for 2-3 minutes till the soup turns thick. Serve hot.

## INGREDIENTS

CHILLI-GARLIC PASTE
½ tsp red chilli paste
½ tsp minced garlic, 1 tbsp oil
OTHER INGREDIENTS
2 tbsp oil
1-2 tender green beans - sliced very finely (3-4 tbsp)
1 tbsp dried mushrooms or 2 fresh mushrooms - chopped
½ cup chopped cabbage
½ cup thickly grated carrot
6 cups water
2 soup/stock cubes - crushed
2 tsp sugar, 1¼ tsp salt
½ tsp pepper powder, or to taste
½- 1 tbsp soya sauce, 2-3 tbsp vinegar
2 tbsp tomato ketchup
6 tbsp cornstarch mixed with ½ cup water

## TiP

**How much Soya Sauce to add?**

*Soya sauce becomes darker in colour and concentrated on keeping. If you have an old bottle of soya sauce lying around, use sparingly and watch the colour of the soup. More can be added later according to the desired colour.*

# Kimchi Salad

*Kimchi is a famous Korean condiment made of pickled cabbage leaves. This salad version captures the authentic flavour for you.*

*Serves 4*

### INGREDIENTS

4 cups cabbage cut into 1" squares, preferably Chinese cabbage
1 tsp salt, ¼ cup vinegar

DRESSING
1 tsp red chilli paste
½ tsp salt, 2 tsp sugar
2 tsp soya sauce, 1 tbsp vinegar
2 tbsp tomato ketchup
1 tbsp red chilli sauce

### METHOD

1 Sprinkle salt and vinegar on cabbage kept in a bowl. Crush cabbage well with the fingers. Keep aside covered for 30 minutes.

2 Strain cabbage. Leave it in the strainer for 15 minutes for the water to drain out completely.

3 Add all ingredients of the dressing to the cabbage. Toss lightly so that the paste coats the cabbage. Let it stand for 30 minutes. Serve at room temperature.

# Chicken Spring Rolls

*These detailed instructions will ensure success every time – because you can't stop eating them!*

*Serves 4*

### INGREDIENTS

**SPRING ROLL WRAPPERS**
½ cup plain flour *(maida)*
¾ cup cornstarch
1 egg white, ½ tsp salt
¼-½ cup water

**FILLING**
1 tbsp oil, ½ tsp minced garlic
1 egg, 1 onion - cut into slices
2 tbsp coriander, ½ tsp salt
½ tsp pepper, 1 tsp soya sauce

**MIX TOGETHER**
150 g/4 oz chicken - cut into thin strips
2 tbsp cornstarch, ½ tsp salt

boiling water and boil for 1 minute. Remove from water. Heat 1 tbsp oil. Add garlic. Stir. Break an egg in it and scramble it quickly for 5-10 seconds. Add onion and coriander, cook for a few seconds. Add boiled chicken, soya sauce, salt and pepper to taste.

### METHOD

**1** To prepare the wrappers, sift plain flour and cornstarch in a mixing bowl. Add egg and beat to break all lumps. Add salt, pepper and enough water to get a thin pouring batter. Leave aside for 15 minutes.

**2** Heat a small non stick pan/skillet with 1 tsp oil. Rub the oil to grease the base of the pan. Remove pan from heat and pour a ladle full of batter. Rotate the pan to cover the base, immediately remove the excess batter in the bowl of batter. This way you avoid getting a thick pancake! Return pan to heat. Cook for about ½ minute, till the sides start to leave the pan. Remove from pan on to a floured surface.

**3** For filling, mix chicken strips with cornstarch and salt. Boil 4 cups water. Add the coated chicken to

**4** To assemble wrapper, spread a pancake on a flat surface. Spread some filling on one edge. Fold in ½" from the right and left sides. Holding on, fold the top part to cover the filling. Roll on to get a rectangular parcel; making sure that all the filling is enclosed.

**5** Seal edges with cornstarch paste, made by dissolving 1 tsp of cornstarch in 1 tsp of water. Chill for ½ hour in the fridge, it gives better shape. Cover all with a plastic wrap/cling film to prevent drying.

**6** Heat some oil in a large frying pan for deep frying. Reduce heat and put the rolls, folded side down first in oil. Turn sides, to make it crisp and golden from all sides. Drain on paper napkins/absorbent paper. Cut into 2 pieces with a sharp knife and serve hot with chilli sauce.

# Steamed Dimsums

*A delicious vegetable filling for these steamed appetisers.*

*Serves 12*

## INGREDIENTS

### WRAPPERS
¾ cup plain flour (*maida*)
¼ cup rice flour or cornstarch
1 tbsp oil, ½ tsp salt

### FILLING
1 onion - finely chopped
6 mushrooms - chopped very finely
1 tsp ginger-garlic paste
2 green chillies - finely chopped
1 large carrot - grated
2½ cups very finely chopped cabbage
1 tsp salt & ½ tsp pepper powder, or to
taste, 1 tbsp vinegar, ½ tsp soya sauce

### RED HOT SAUCE
2-3 dry, red chillies - desseded & soaked
in ¼ cup warm water for 10 minutes
6-8 flakes garlic, 1 tsp coriander seeds
1 tsp cumin seeds (*jeera*), 1 tbsp oil
½ tsp salt, 1 tsp sugar
2-3 tbsp vinegar, ½ tsp soya sauce

## METHOD

1. Sift maida, cornstarch and salt together. Add oil and knead with enough water to make a stiff dough of rolling consistency. Keep in a cool place covered with a cling wrap for 30 minutes.

2. Heat 2 tbsp oil in wok for the filling. Add the chopped onion. Fry till it turns soft. Add mushrooms and cook further for 2 minutes. Add green chillies, carrot, cabbage & ginger-garlic paste. Stir fry on high flame for 3 minutes. Add salt, pepper, vinegar and soya to taste. Remove from heat and keep the filling aside to cool.

3. Take out the dough and form marble sized small balls. Roll out flat, as thin as possible into small rounds of 2½" diameter.

4. Put 1 heaped tsp of the filling on one side and fold over to form a semicircle. Stick the edges with water. Pleat the joint edges and then slightly fold the pointed ends to give it a little rounded shape. Make all dimsums. Steam for 10 minutes.

5. For chutney, grind the soaked red chillies along with the water, garlic, coriander seeds, cumin, oil, salt and sugar to a paste. Add soya sauce and vinegar to taste.

4a

4b

# Corn Rolls

*A slice of bread is a short-cut to making these sesame crusted rolls.*

*Makes 16 pieces*

**2** Add garlic and green chilli and stir for a second on medium heat. Add 1 cup cream style sweet corn. Mix well and cook for a minute. Add tomato ketchup, salt, pepper and vinegar. Cook for 2 minutes till almost dry. Remove from heat Cool.

**3** Cut the sides of a slice, keep if flat on a rolling board. Press, applying pressure with a rolling pin so that the holes of the bread close. Keep aside. Similarly roll the other slices.

**4** Mix cornstarch with water in a wide dish, big enough to hold the complete roll.

**5** Spread a layer of the filling on each bread. Roll bread carefully. Stick the end using the cornstarch paste. Cut edges of the roll to neaten them, if required.

**6** Scatter 1 tbsp white sesame seeds and ½ tsp black sesame seeds on a plate.

**7** Dip the roll in cornstarch batter and roll over sesame seeds. Wrap in a cling wrap or foil till serving.

**8** To serve, pan fry/deep fry each roll in hot oil till golden. See that the roll turns a nice golden before you remove from oil so that the bread is crisp. Cut each roll into 4 pieces with a bread knife and serve hot.

## INGREDIENTS

4 slices of fresh bread

**FILLING**
2 tbsp oil, ½ cup finely chopped onion
½ tsp crushed garlic
1 green chilli - deseeded & chopped
1 cup cream style sweet corn, (buy a tin, store the rest in the freezer)
1 tsp tomato ketchup, ½ tsp salt
¼ tsp pepper to taste, 1 tsp vinegar

**COATING**
3 tbsp cornstarch, ¼ cup water
1 tbsp white sesame seeds
½ tsp black sesame seeds

## METHOD

**1** Heat oil in a pan, add onion. Cook till onion turns golden.

# Golden Fried Prawns

*Tender and juicy prawns – crisp on the outside!*

*Serves 4*

## INGREDIENTS

(250 g/8 oz) 12 large shrimps/prawns -
cleaned & deveined, 1 tsp lemon juice
½ tsp salt, 2 tbsp cornstarch

### MARINADE
1 tsp soya sauce, 1 tbsp wine or sherry
½ tbsp vinegar
1 tsp salt, ¼ tsp pepper

### BATTER
1 egg white, 3 tbsp cornstarch
a pinch baking powder
¼ tsp white pepper, ½ tsp salt
1 tbsp oil, 1 tbsp sesame seeds

## METHOD

1. Wash prawns. Rub them well with lemon juice and salt. Keep aside for 15 minutes. Wash and pat dry.

2. In a bowl mix all ingredients of the marinade. Marinate the prawns in it for at least one hour in the fridge.

3. Mix all ingredients of the batter till smooth.

4. Pick up the prawns from the marinade and pat dry. Roll over a little cornstarch spread out in a plate. Dip the prawns in batter

5. Heat oil. Reduce heat and put 5-6 prawns at a time in oil. Fry for 2-3 minutes on medium heat. Serve hot with chilli sauce.

**Note:** *If desired you can marinate the shrimps/prawns without removing the tail.*

# Saucy Dishes

# Veggies in Szechwan Sauce

*The Szechwan region of China makes generous use of red chillies. Here 7 different vegetables as well as tofu or paneer are tossed in a red hot sauce.*

*Serves 4*

## INGREDIENTS

100 g/3 oz tofu or paneer - cut into triangles
4-5 florets of broccoli or cauliflower
4-6 babycorns - cut into 2 pieces diagonally
1 carrot - sliced diagonally
6-8 leaves of bokchoy or spinach
2-3 dried black mushrooms or fresh mushrooms
1 bell pepper - cut into 1" pieces
2 tbsp bamboo shoots (tinned) - cut into thin diagonal slices

### SZECHWAN SAUCE
4 tbsp oil
1 tbsp minced garlic
1 tsp chilli paste
1 onion- cut into 1" pieces
2 cloves (*laung*) - crushed
3 tbsp ready-made tomato puree
2 tbsp tomato ketchup
1 tsp red chilli sauce
2 tsp soya sauce
¼ tsp pepper
½ tsp salt or to taste
1 tsp sugar, or to taste
1½ cups water
2 soup/stock cubes
3 tbsp cornstarch mixed with ½ cup water

## METHOD

1. If using dried black mushrooms, put them in a pan. Cover with water. Boil. Simmer for 2 minutes. Remove from heat. Keep aside for 10 minutes. Wash several times. Break off any hard stem portion and discard. Wash several times scrubbing well, to clean the hidden dirt. Cut into pieces.

2. If using bokchoy or spinach, trim the stem, remove any discoloured leaves. Tear into 2" pieces.

5    To prepare the sauce, heat 2 tbsp oil again in the same pan. Remove from heat. Add garlic and red chilli paste. Stir till garlic starts to change its colour.

6    Add onion. Saute for 1 minute. Add cloves, tomato puree, ketchup, red chilli sauce, Soya sauce, pepper, salt and sugar. Cook for 1 minute on low heat.

7    Add water mixed with seasoning cubes, give one boil.

8    Add cornstarch paste, stirring all the time. Cook for 2 minutes on low heat. Add bamboo shoots. Remove from heat. Keep aside till serving time.

9    To serve, heat the sauce. Add the soaked mushrooms, tofu, blanched vegetables and bell pepper. Bring to a boil and simmer for 1 minute. Serve.

3    Boil 4-5 cups water with 1 tsp salt. Remove from heat. Add broccoli or cauliflower, baby corns, carrots and bokchoy or spinach. Leave veggies in hot water for 1-2 minutes and strain. Refresh in cold water and keep aside till serving time.

4    Heat 4 tbsp oil in a pan. Shallow fry the tofu till golden. Remove tofu from pan.

# American Chopsuey with Vegetables

*Crisp-fried noodles will absorb sauce and turn limp if mixed with the vegetables too much in advance – so assemble the dish only just before serving and experience the wonderful crunch of these noodles!*

*Serves 4*

## INGREDIENTS

**CRISPY NOODLES**
125 g/4 oz noodles
1 tbsp cornstarch
2 cups oil for frying

**VEGETABLES IN SAUCE**
1 carrot - shredded
8 green beans or snow peas
1 bell pepper - shredded
1 onion - shredded
¾ cup cabbage - shredded
½ cup long bean sprouts
2 cups water
½ tsp white pepper, salt to taste
3 tbsp oil
1 tsp soya sauce, 1 tsp vinegar
4 tbsp tomato ketchup
3 tbsp cornstarch dissolved in ½ cup water

## METHOD

1   To prepare crispy noodles, boil noodles till slightly soft. Strain and refresh in cold. Leave in the strainer for all water to drip off. Sprinkle 1 tsp oil on the noodles and spread out on a tray for 15 minutes to dry. Sprinkle cornstarch on noodles to absorb any water present.

2   Heat about 2 cups of oil. Add half of the noodles. Stir, turning sides till noodles are golden in colour and form a nest like appearance. Remove from oil. Drain on absorbent paper. Fry the remaining noodles in the same way. Cool and use or store in an air tight tin till further use.

3   Scrape carrot, string green beans or snow peas. Shred all vegetables into thin long strips - bell pepper, onion, cabbage, carrot and green beans or snow peas.

4   Heat 3 tbsp of oil. Except sprouts add all the remaining vegetables. Stir fry for 2-3 minutes.

**5** Add sprouts, pepper and salt. Stir fry for 1 minute.

**6** Add soya sauce, vinegar and tomato ketchup. Cook for ½ minute.

**7** Add 2 cups water. Bring to a boil.

**8** Add cornstarch paste, stirring continuously. Cook for about 2 minutes, till thick. Keep aside.

**9** To serve, spread crispy noodles on a serving platter, keeping aside a few for the top.

**10** Top with the prepared vegetables.

**11** Sprinkle the remaining crispy noodles on top. Serve hot.

# Sweet and Sour Vegetables

*This easy recipe makes a winner every time.*

*Serves 4*

## INGREDIENTS

1 carrot - cut into diagonal slices
4-5 medium florets cauliflowers
6-7 slices of cucumber
1 small bell pepper - cut into ½" pieces
2 slices tinned pineapple
½ cup pineapple syrup or juice
2 tbsp oil
1-2 green onions - cut into slices
½ tsp red chilli paste
1½ tsp roughly crushed or minced garlic
¼ cup tomato ketchup
5 tbsp vinegar
½ tsp soya sauce
4 tsp sugar
½ tsp salt or to taste
1 stock/soup cube - crushed
3 tbsp cornstarch mixed in ¼ cup water

2  Add tomato ketchup, vinegar, soya sauce, sugar, salt and stock-cube. Keep aside.

3  Heat 2 tbsp oil in a wok. Add white of onions, garlic and red chilli paste. Stir for a minute.

4  Add remaining vegetables - cucumber, pineapple and bell pepper. Stir for a minute.

5  Add the vegetables in pineapple syrup to the wok. Bring to a boil.

6  Add cornstarch paste, stirring all the time. Cook for 2 minutes on low heat. Serve hot with rice or noodles.

## METHOD

1  Boil 1½ cups water with ½ cup pineapple juice. Add carrot and cauliflower. Boil for 2 minutes.

# Spicy Ginger Honey Fish

*Batter-fried fish in a delicate sauce – you will love it!*

*Serves 3-4*

## INGREDIENTS

150 g/4 oz sliced fish (boneless) - cut into 1" pieces
½ tsp salt, 1 tbsp lemon juice

### BATTER
½ tsp salt
1 tbsp ginger-garlic paste
4 tbsp egg, about 1 egg
2 tbsp cornstarch, 2 tbsp flour (*maida*)
1 tbsp red chilli paste

### VEGETABLES
½ bell pepper - cut into 1" cubes
¼ red bell pepper - cut into 1" cubes
¼ yellow bell pepper - cut into 1" cubes
1 green onion - sliced thickly and diagonally, including the greens
2 fresh red chillies - cut diagonally into 1" length

### SAUCE
1 tbsp oil, 1 tsp minced ginger
1 tsp red chilli paste
250 ml/8 oz stock (1 cup)
1 tsp salt
1 tbsp honey
a pinch of red colour, 1 tsp white vinegar
4 tbsp cornstarch mixed with ½ cup water/stock
1 tsp ginger juice (grate a piece of ginger and squeeze)

## METHOD

1 Wash fish well. Rub salt and lemon juice on the fish. Keep in the fridge for ½ hour. Wash and pat dry.

2 Make a batter of coating consistency with all the ingredients of the batter.

3 Dip fish in batter and deep fry till for 1-2 minutes on medium heat. Check for doneness. The fish should turn white and flaky. It should not be pink from inside. Keep fried fish aside.

4 Heat 1 tbsp oil in a wok, add chopped ginger and stir for a few seconds.

5 Add the vegetables and the chilli paste. Stir again for a few seconds.

6 Add stock, salt, honey, colour and vinegar. Stir to mix well.

7 Add the fried fish.

8 Add cornstarch paste and mix well. Let the sauce come to a boil. Simmer for ½ minute. Remove from heat and add ginger juice. Mix well and serve hot with rice or noodles.

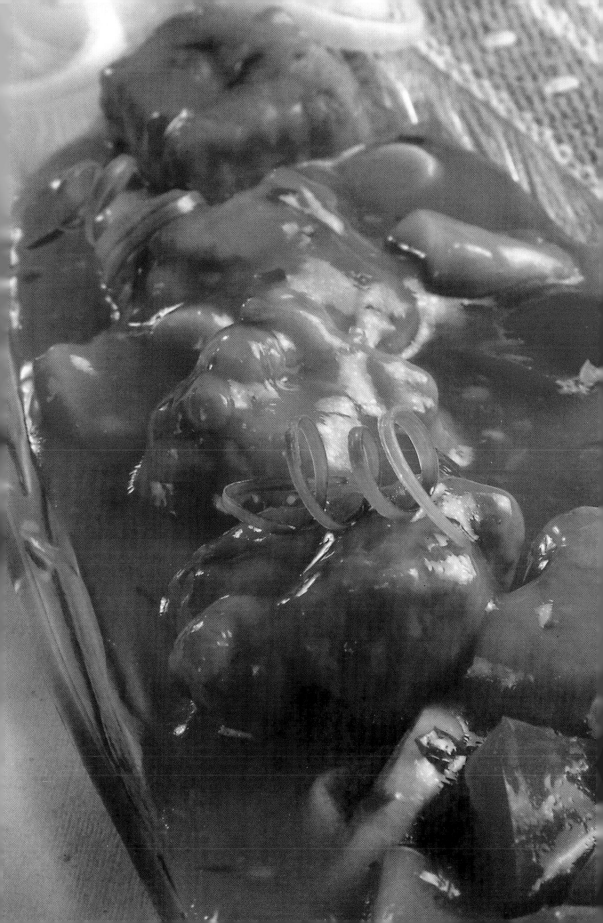

# Chicken in Black Pepper Sauce

*Delectable chicken morsels are carefully seasoned with black pepper.*

*Serves 4*

1 Cut chicken into 1" pieces. Marinate the chicken in all the ingredients of the marinade and keep aside for at least ½ hour.

2 Heat oil in a wok or a kadhai and deep fry the chicken for 2-3 minutes on medium heat. Drain and keep aside. Do not let the chicken be in the oil for a longer time as it gets overcooked and turns hard.

3 For the sauce, heat 2 tbsp oil. Reduce heat add ginger, garlic and peppercorns. Cook till garlic starts to change colour. Add black pepper, soya sauce, vinegar and fried chicken.

4 Add water mixed with cube or chicken stock. Add enough water (½ cup approx.) mixed with cornstarch. Cook stirring till it turns to a thick saucy consistency. Add salt to taste.

5 Add greens of green onion. Remove from heat. Serve hot.

## INGREDIENTS

200 g/6 oz chicken (boneless) - cut into 1" pieces
greens of 1 green onion - cut into ½" pieces

### SAUCE
2 tbsp oil
½ tsp peppercorns (*saboot kali mirch*)
½ tsp chopped garlic, ½ tsp ginger paste
1 tsp freshly ground black pepper
½ -1 tsp soya sauce, 1 tsp vinegar
1½ cups water mixed with 1 chicken soup cube
OR
1½ cups chicken stock/broth
4 tbsp cornstarch

### MARINADE
1 egg, ½ tsp salt, 2 tbsp cornstarch
2 tbsp flour (*maida*)

# Chicken in Hot Garlic Sauce

*A treat for garlic lovers and chicken lovers as well!*

*Serves 4*

## INGREDIENTS

200 g/6 oz boneless chicken - cut into
1" cubes
1 tbsp oil, 1 tbsp chopped garlic
½ green bell pepper - cut into ½" cubes
1 green onion - sliced diagonally
1½ cups chicken stock or water mixed
with 1 soup cube
salt to taste
½ tsp sugar
1 tsp red chilli paste
1 tbsp vinegar
1½ tbsp tomato ketchup
2 tsp soya sauce
3 tbsp cornstarch

### MARINADE

1 egg, 1 tsp salt, 1 tbsp crushed garlic
2 tbsp cornstarch, 2 tbsp flour (*maida*)

## METHOD

1 Cut the chicken breast into even sized pieces. Marinate the chicken in all the ingredients of the marinade and keep aside for at least ½ hour.

2 Heat oil in a wok. Deep fry the chicken for 2-3 minutes on medium heat till very light golden. Drain and keep aside. Do not let the chicken be in the oil for a longer time as it gets overcooked and turns hard.

3 For the sauce, heat 1 tbsp oil. Reduce heat add white part of green onion and garlic. Add bell peppers. Stir.

4 Add stock, salt, sugar, chilli paste, vinegar, tomato ketchup and soya sauce. Let it come to a boil.

5 Add chicken and mix well.

6 Add enough water (½ cup approx.) mixed with cornstarch. Cook stirring till it turns to a thick saucy consistency.

7 Add greens of green onion. Remove from heat. Serve hot.

# Dry &
# Stir Fried

# Dry Chilli Chicken

*A no-fuss, easy-to-make-dish – what a boon for the busy cook!*

*Serves 4*

## INGREDIENTS

300 g/10 oz chicken - cut into pieces
2 tbsp oil
6-8 green chillies - slit lengthwise
1 tbsp crushed garlic
½ onion - cut into 1" pieces
½ green bell pepper - cut into 1" pieces
½ tsp sugar
½ tsp salt, ¼ tsp pepper
1 tsp red chilli paste
3 tsp soya sauce, 1½ tbsp vinegar
3 tbsp tomato ketchup
2 tbsp cornstarch mixed with ¼ cup
stock/water

## MARINADE

1 egg, 1 tsp salt, 1 tbsp crushed garlic
2 tbsp cornstarch
2 tbsp flour (*maida*)

## METHOD

1 Cut the chicken into even sized pieces. Marinate the chicken in all the ingredients of the marinade and keep aside for at least ½ hour.

2 Heat oil in a wok. Deep fry the chicken for 2-3 minutes on medium heat till very light golden. Drain and keep aside. Do not let the chicken be in the oil for a longer time as it gets overcooked and turns hard.

3 Heat 2 tbsp oil. Fry green chillies lightly and remove.

4 Heat the remaining oil. Reduce heat add onion and garlic. Stir. Add bell peppers. Stir for 2 minutes.

5 Add salt, pepper, sugar, chilli paste, soya sauce, vinegar and tomato ketchup. Stir.

6 Add cornstarch paste. Stir. Add chicken and mix well. Add green chillies. Stir well to get the chicken coated with sauces.

# Spicy Honey Veggies

*A colourful and crunchy vegetable medley lightly coated with honey-flavoured sauce.*

*Serves 4*

## INGREDIENTS

1 large carrot, 5-6 mushrooms - trim
stalks and keep whole
4-5 baby corns - cut lengthwise
½ cup broccoli florets- cut into small,
flat florets, 1 cup cauliflower florets
1 onion - cut into 8 pieces and separated
1 bell pepper - cut into ½" cubes
4 tbsp oil
1-2 dry, red chillies - broken into bits &
deseeded
1 tbsp crushed
¾ tsp salt and ¼ tsp pepper, or to taste
2-3 tsp red chilli sauce
2½ tbsp tomato ketchup
1 tsp soya sauce, 1½ tbsp vinegar
3-4 tsp honey, according to taste
3 tbsp cornstarch, ½ cup water
1 soup cube

## METHOD

1 Boil 4 cups water with 1 tsp salt. Peel carrot. Drop the whole carrot, mushroom, cauliflower and baby corns in boiling water. Boil for a minute, remove from heat and strain the vegetables. Refresh veggies in cold water.

2 Cut blanched carrot into ¼" thick round slices or flowers. To make flowers, make slits or grooves along the length of the boiled carrot, leaving a little space between the slits. Cut the grooved carrot widthwise into slices to get flowers.

3 Dissolve cornstarch in ½ cup water. Add soup cube and keep aside.

4 Heat 4 tbsp oil in a wok. Reduce heat. Add broken red chillies and garlic.

5 Stir and add onion, mushroom, baby corns, carrots and cauliflower. Add salt and pepper. Stir for 1-2 minutes on high flame. Add bell pepper. Reduce heat.

6 Add chilli sauce, tomato ketchup, soya sauce, honey & vinegar. Lower heat & stir for ½ minute.

7 Add the cornstarch paste. Cook till the vegetables are crisp-tender and the sauce coats the veggies.

## TiP

***How much soya sauce to add?***
*Soya sauce adds colour too, besides enhancing flavour. Different types of soya sauce are available - dark & light. Also, if the soya sauce has been lying around in the house for a few months, it gets concentrated and even a small quantity of it, imparts a dark colour to the food. It is always better to add a lesser quantity of the sauce and add more later according to the colour of the dish. Too much soya sauce spoils the colour of the dish sometimes!*

# Hoisin Stir Fry Okra

*Keep the batter-fried okra ready. Just before serving toss it in hoisin sauce – the okra will retain its crunch. Hoisin sauce is commercially available, but can be replaced by tomato ketchup if necessary.*

*Serves 4*

## INGREDIENTS

250 g/8 oz okra (*bhindi*) - slice into 2
pieces lengthwise
1 onion - cut into 8 pieces
1 tbsp oil, 1 tsp ginger-garlic paste
2-3 tbsp Hoisin sauce
1 tbsp soya sauce
2 tbsp red chilli sauce, ¼ tsp salt
1 tbsp cornstarch mixed with ¼ cup water
oil for frying

### THIN COATING BATTER
½ cup cornstarch
2 tbsp plain flour (*maida*)
1 tsp ginger-garlic paste, ½ tsp salt
¼ tsp white pepper powder
1 tsp soya sauce, ½ tsp vinegar
1 tsp lemon juice
¼ cup water, approx.

## METHOD

1. Wash and wipe dry okra with a clean napkin. Cut into 2 long pieces lengthwise.

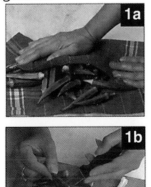

2. Mix all ingredients of the batter in a big bowl, adding enough cold water (about ¼ to ½ cup) to get a coating batter of pouring consistency. Do not make the batter too thick or too thin.

3. Dip the okra in batter and mix well. The batter should coat the vegetable lightly. If not, sprinkle 2 tbsp more cornstarch on the vegetable and mix well. Deep fry in hot oil till pale golden on medium heat. Remove on paper napkin. Keep aside till serving time.

4. Heat 1 tbsp oil in a pan and stir fry onions for 2 minutes.

5. Add the ginger-garlic paste and saute for half a minute.

6. Shut off the heat, add the hoisin sauce, soya sauce, red chilli sauce and ¼ tsp salt. Mix well and keep aside till serving time.

7. At serving time, return to heat and add the cornstarch paste. Add fried okra. Mix gently for a minute. Serve immediately.

### TiP
*Stir frying takes only few minutes Deep fry okra and keep aside till serving time. Stir fry the fried okra with sauces at the time of serving.*

*Hoisin sauce makes an excellent base for dips. Mix it with seasonings and try it.*

# Stir fried Snow Peas/Beans

*This quick stir-fry uses tofu or paneer combined with any seasonal vegetables that are handy – the simplest version could use only green onions.*

*Serves 4*

### METHOD

1   Remove strings/threads from snow peas or beans.

2   If using snow peas, keep whole. If using green beans, cut each into 1½-2" pieces. If using beans, boil 4-5 cups water with 1 tsp salt and 1 tsp sugar. Add beans and boil for 1-2 minutes. Strain.

3   Peel onion. Cut into half and then cut widthwise to get half rings, which when opened become thin long strips and you get shredded onion.

4   Cut tofu/paneer into fingers.

5   Heat 4 tbsp oil in pan. Add onion, cook till golden.

6   Add ginger jullienes and green chillies. Stir fry for 1-2 minutes till ginger turns golden.

7   Add snow peas or beans and stir fry for 3-4 minutes till vegetable turns crisp-tender. Keep the vegetable spread out in the pan while stir frying.

8   Reduce heat. Add soya sauce, tomato ketchup, vinegar, red chilli sauce, sherry, Worcestershire sauce, salt and pepper.

9   Add tofu/paneer and mix well. Stir fry on low heat for 2 minutes till the vegetables blend well with the sauces.  Serve hot.

### TiP
**Snow Peas/Mangetout:**
*They belong to the pea family and are used in cooking just like we use Green beans. Whole pod is edible. Snap off the stem end of pea pod and pull the thread.*

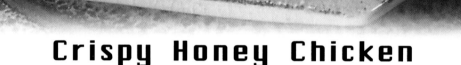

# Crispy Honey Chicken

*The secret is to slightly freeze the chicken so that it can be cut very thinly – deep-fry chicken strips till crisp then toss in a tongue-tingling sauce.*

*Serves 3-4*

## INGREDIENTS

2 chicken breast (300 g/10 oz) - frozen for 30 minutes and sliced very thinly

### BATTER
2 egg whites (discard yolks)
2 tbsp oil, 6 tbsp cornstarch
1¼ tsp salt ½ tsp white pepper

### OTHER INGREDIENTS
2 tbsp oil
1-2 dry red chillies - cut diagonally into 1" pieces
1-2 green onions - white part thickly sliced diagonally and the greens cut into 1" long pieces, ½ tsp soya sauce
4 tbsp tomato ketchup, 5-6 tbsp honey
¼ - ½ cup stock or water
¼ tsp salt, or to taste
2 tbsp cornstarch dissolved in ¼ cup water
2 tsp sesame seeds

## METHOD

1. Mix all ingredients of the batter and put chicken in it. Deep fry putting one piece at a time in the oil, so that they do not stick to each other. Deep fry in 2 batches till light and crispy, keeping them in oil for about 4 minutes. Keep aside.

2. Heat 2 tbsp oil in a wok. Put red chillies and the green onion whites. Stir for a minute.

3. Add the soya sauce, tomato ketchup, honey, stock, salt & mix well.

4. Add cornstarch paste. Add the chicken & 1 tsp sesame seeds & toss well to coat each piece of chicken evenly.

5. Serve hot garnished with 1 tsp sesame seeds.

# Noodles & Rice

# Chilli Garlic Noodles

*You won't find veggies in these stir-fried noodles because they are meant to accompany a sauce-based main dish.*

*Serves 3-4*

## INGREDIENTS

200 g/ 6 oz noodles
3 tbsp oil, 1 tsp crushed garlic
3 dry, whole red chillies - broken into bits
½ tsp red chilli flakes
½ tsp salt or to taste
1 tsp soya sauce

## METHOD

1. To boil noodles, boil a deep pan with 8-10 cups water. Add 2 tsp salt and 1 tbsp oil to it. Add noodles to boiling water. Stir with a fork. Boil till just done, for about 1-2 minutes only. Remove from heat. Strain after a minute. Leave in the strainer for all the water to drip off, for about 15 minutes. Sprinkle 1 tbsp oil on them and mix lightly. Spread on a tray and keep aside for 1 hour to dry out.

2. Cut the dry red chillies into small bits or pieces.

3. Heat 2 tbsp oil. Add garlic. Stir.

4. Remove from heat, add broken red chillies and red chilli flakes.

5. Return to heat and mix in the boiled noodles. Add salt and a little soya sauce. Do not add too much soya sauce.

6. Mix well with the help of 2 forks. Fry for 2-3 minutes, till the noodles turn a pale brown. Serve hot.

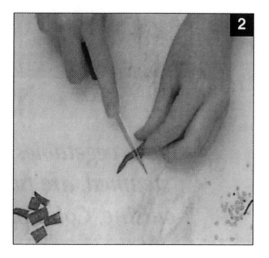

### TiP

*By drizzling soy sauce from the sides of the wok, a savory aroma will be released and enhance the flavor.*

# Shrimp Egg Rice

*Shrimps and thinly cut veggies are scrambled along with eggs then stirred with cooked rice – ready to eat in no time at all!*

*Serves 4*

## INGREDIENTS

2 cups rice, 1 tsp lime juice
2 eggs
200 g/6 oz cleaned shrimps (very small prawns)
3 tbsp oil
½ onion - finely chopped
¼ cup very finely sliced green beans
1 carrot - cut into tiny cubes
¼ cup peas - boiled or frozen
1 tsp salt
¼ tsp pepper, a pinch of sugar
½ tsp soya sauce

## METHOD

1   Wash rice & boil in salted water till just done. Strain to drain excess water. Fluff rice in the strainer with a fork. Transfer to a big tray to cool. Separate the grains with a fork.

2   Squeeze lime juice oven the rice & cool under a fan for 5-7 minutes.

3   Beat eggs in a bowl and season with a pinch of salt and pepper.

4   Heat the wok and add 3 tbsp oil. Add beaten eggs and scramble it quickly.

5   Add onions and shrimps. Stir for 1-2 minutes. Add beans, carrots and peas. Stir for 2 minutes.

6   Add rice, salt, pepper and sugar. Stir in soya sauce and mix well. Serve hot.

# Dessert

# Toffee Apples

*Apple pieces are dipped in batter, deep-fried & coated in caramel syrup & sesame seeds.*

*Serves 4-6*

## INGREDIENTS

2 apples
1 cup oil for deep frying

BATTER
¼ cup plain flour (*maida*)
½ cup cornstarch
½ tsp baking powder
1 tsp sugar, 1 tbsp oil
½ cup water, approx.

CARAMEL COATING
1 cup sugar
1½ cups water
1 tbsp sesame (*til*) seeds

## METHOD

1  For the caramel coating, boil sugar and water together in a non stick skillet on medium flame till it attains a one-string consistency, for about 20 minutes. Do not discolour the syrup. Remove from heat.

2  When the mixture begins to bubble, stir continuously to prevent the sugar from burning.

3  Continue stirring the pan until the syrup is light brown in colour and feels sticky when felt between the thumb and the fore finger. It forms a thread when the finger is pulled apart.

4  Remove from the heat. Keep the caramel syrup aside.

5  Mix all batter ingredients in a bowl. Add enough water to get a smooth, thick batter of a coating consistency.

6  Peel and cut each apple into four pieces. Remove the seeds. Cut each piece into 3 pieces lengthwise.

7  Heat 1 cup oil for frying. Coat the apple pieces evenly with the batter and deep fry on medium heat till golden brown. Let the apples be in oil for another 2 minutes to turn crisp. Drain on kitchen towel.

8  Keep a serving bowl filled with ice-cubes ready and cover with water.

9  Put the fried apples in the caramel syrup and coat evenly. Sprinkle sesame seeds and mix. Drain well and dip immediately into the ice-cubes bowl. Keep for a minute till the caramel coating hardens.

10  Drain thoroughly. Keep aside till serving time. Serve plain or with ice cream.

# GLOSSARY OF NAMES/TERMS

| | |
|---|---|
| **Al dente** | Noodles and vegetables should be cooked to a texture that is not too soft; it should be 'firm to bite' which in Italian is 'al dente'. |
| **Basil** | A fragrant herb |
| **Baste** | To brush food with fat to prevent it from drying out. |
| **Bean Curd** | See tofu |
| **Blanch** | To remove skin by dipping into hot water for a couple of minutes. e.g. to blanch tomatoes or almonds. |
| **Blend** | To combine two or more ingredients. |
| **Bell Pepper** | Capsicum |
| **Cilantro** | See coriander |
| **Coriander, fresh** | A green herb. All parts of the plant are flavourful and hence edible - leaves, stalks and the Thai also use the root of coriander. Also called cilantro in the west. |
| **Cornflour** | Cornstarch |
| **Chutney, (mango)** | Condiment of fruit, vinegar and spices |
| **Dice** | To cut into small neat cubes. |
| **Dough** | A mixture of flour, liquid etc., kneaded together into a stiff paste or roll. |
| **Drain** | To remove liquid from food. |
| **Garnish** | To decorate. |
| **Fish Sauce** | A fermented sauce prepared from small fish |
| **Green Onion** | Spring onions, scallions |
| **Galangal** | Thai ginger |
| **Green Beans** | Also called French beans. The tender variety should be used. |
| **Juliennes** | To cut into thin long pieces, like match sticks. |
| **Kaffir Lime** | A variety of lime found in Thailand |
| **Lemon Grass** | Imparts a lemony flavour to the food |
| **Marinate** | To soak food in a mixture for some time so that the flavour of the mixture penetrates into the food. |
| **Paneer** | The Indian cheese prepared from milk. |
| **Plain Flour** | All purpose flour, *maida*. |
| **Red Chilli Powder** | Cayenne pepper |
| **Rind** | The outer skin of citrous fruits like lemon, orange etc. |
| **Saute** | To toss and make light brown in shallow fat. |
| **Shred** | To cut into thin, long pieces. |
| **Sift** | To pass dry ingredients through a fine sieve. |
| **Snow Peas** | The whole flat green pods are edible; the peas are not fully formed. |
| **Star Anise** | A star-shaped, fennel-flavoured fruit, dried and used as a spice. |
| **Tofu** | Cheese prepared from soya bean milk. Also called bean curd. |
| **Turmeric** | A yellow spice with antiseptic properties. Usually available as a powder. It imparts a yellow colour to food. |
| **Toss** | To lightly mix ingredients without mashing them e.g. salads. |